Martina Steinkühler • Barbara Nascimbeni

Prayers

FOR YOUNG CHILDREN

Translated by Laura Watkinson

Eerdmans Books for Young Readers

Grand Rapids, Michigan

Martina Steinkühler is a professor of religious education at the Protestant College in Berlin. She is also a freelance writer and lecturer, and often speaks at seminars on biblical narratives and religious education. She lives with her family in Germany.

Barbara Nascimbeni was born in Italy and studied illustration in Italy and Germany. She has illustrated numerous children's books, including *Our Father* and *Images of God for Young Children* (both Eerdmans). She currently splits her time between Germany and France. Visit her website at www.barbaranascimbeni.com.

This edition published in 2018 by
Eerdmans Books for Young Readers,
an imprint of William B. Eerdmans Publishing Co.
2140 Oak Industrial Dr. NE, Grand Rapids, Michigan 49505

www.eerdmans.com/youngreaders

Originally published in Germany under the title *Für dich bin ich immer da—Gebete für Kinder*
© 2016 by Gabriel in Thienemann-Esslinger GmbH, Stuttgart

Manufactured in China

27 26 25 24 23 22 21 20 19 18   1 2 3 4 5 6 7 8 9

ISBN 978-0-8028-5493-3

A catalog record of this book is available from the Library of Congress.

Introduction

Praying and seeking guidance come naturally to us. When we're young, we turn to our parents for help and instincitvely cry out "Mommy!" or "Daddy!" And similarly, we turn to God and say, "Please, God!" and "Thank you, God!" Those are our first prayers, and the most common ones. But it can still feel hard to pray sometimes. Perhaps that's because we don't always feel close to God. And that can make us ask questions like these:

- What does God want to hear?
- What should I say? What shouldn't I say?
- Are there words I have to use to make it a "real" prayer?
- Will God hear me?
- Does praying actually help?

The prayers in this book were inspired by Bible stories and the Psalms. The people in the Bible knew all about life and what it means to be human. The relationship they had with God helped them understand the good and bad in their lives. The Psalms express so many of our life experiences: celebrating and complaining, doubting, pleading, and being grateful.

When people pray, they can find out how it might help them. This collection of prayers is an invitation. No matter how you're feeling right now or what's on your mind, take it to God. You'll soon see how much it can help.

These prayers are organized according to emotions and experiences, both big and small, under keywords such as "Amazement," "Guilt," and "Frustration." You can go through the book in order, or just open it to any page and read! At the end of the book, there's an index highlighting the Bible passages that inspired these prayers.

Contents

Fear . . . of the dark and nighttime

I can't get to sleep
Pray like Abraham when God called him into a new land

Do you hear me, God,
way up there in heaven?
They've told me all about you.
But do you know me?

It is dark.
It is night.
My parents tell me
I shouldn't be afraid.
They say that a lot.

I'm not a baby anymore.
But deep inside
I am afraid.
Could you make
the night
a little bit
lighter
for me,
God?

I am reassured

Pray like Abraham when God made a covenant with him

Dear God,
the night was still dark.
And yet I believe that
you heard me!

You took away my fear
in the night.
I fell asleep
peacefully
and woke up happy,
with the sun
tickling my nose.

They say you made the day
and the night.
The moon, the stars,
and the sun.

And me, you made me, too!
Thank you.
You designed it all so well.
You made everything,
and you made it all so well!

Fear ... of new things

I am uncertain
Pray like Moses when God gave him a big job to do

God in heaven,
do you hear me?

I have a wish.
I want you to walk beside me
and take good care of me.

Because, you see,
I have to take a big step,
and no one else can do this for me.
Not even you—I know that.

You won't take any of this weight from me,
but you can make it easier to carry
if you walk with me, God.

You say to me:
I am who I am,
and I am there for you.

Let it be so, God!
Be who you are,
and be there for me too.

I am in a new situation

Pray like Daniel when he
arrived in Babylon

Dear God,
why am I here?
I didn't choose this—
this new city,
these new people,
this whole mess
at home.

Dear God,
I want to go back.
I want everything to be
like it was before.
It was good back then.

I take courage

Pray like Daniel when he made the best of things

Dear God,
I realize that there is no going back.

And there is no going forward either—
until I decide that I'm ready to move on.
They say it's up to me,
that I need to "open up."
Open up to all the new things.

11

Dear God, do you think that too?
They say you know all my thoughts.

What would it be like, God,
if I could actually be open
to face all this mess?

You know, I'm starting to feel a little curious!
I think I'll give it a try.

Loneliness . . . at school

I am looking for a friend
Pray like Zacchaeus when he was alone

God, my companion,
I am lying in my bed,
and it's getting late.
But I can't sleep a wink.

The day is still replaying
over and over in my head.
School, recess,
fighting, shouting.
And the teacher says I'm always
right in the middle of things.

But, God, you know me.
You know that's only how it looks
from the outside.
Inside, I feel so alone.
Don't hold it against me.
Of course, I know that I have you.
And Mom and the rest of my family.

But there's no other way
to say it:
Inside, I feel alone.

Jesus, let me find a friend,
someone who will stand by my side.
My friend doesn't have to be
smart or brave.
As long as we like each other
and can help each other.

Let me find a friend,
someone who will stand by my side.
My friend doesn't have to be
cool or popular.
As long as we like each other
and can help each other.

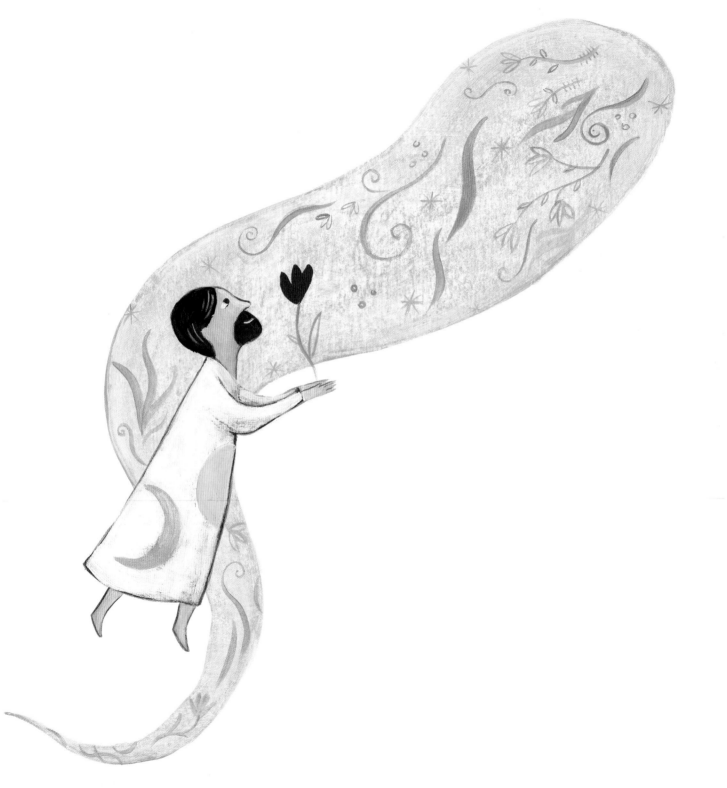

I am new

Pray like Ruth when she first arrived in Bethlehem

God, great Father in heaven.
Jesus, you are God among us.
Holy Spirit, you connect all people.

Please hear me:
I'm new at this school
and new in this class.
I feel so strange,
so scared and shaky.
I don't like standing here alone.

I imagine
coming to school
and someone smiling at me and saying,
"Hey, where are you from?
I'm glad you're here."

Thank God, I would think,
and I would smile back. *Thank God,*
you were sent by heaven.

I am persistent

Pray like Paul when he encouraged believers to be welcoming

Well, God,
this isn't easy!
Standing and looking and waiting,
hoping someone will speak to me . . .
No, it isn't easy!

I need your courage, God,
to talk to them,
the other kids who just stand and stare at me,
and to ask one of them, "Will you help me?"

I need your strength, God,
to go up to the kids who turn away.
To ask them to get to know me.

God, I know it won't happen by itself,
and it won't happen all at once.

I'll need more courage and strength.
And patience too.

Frustration . . . about wasted effort

I am disappointed
Pray like Sarah when Hagar had the child that Sarah wanted so much

Dear God,
this feels so unfair.
Why did it all go wrong?
I really wanted everything to turn out well.
I tried so hard.
And I prayed.
But maybe you didn't hear me.

Or maybe . . .
Were you unable to help me?
Did you not want to help me?

Forgive me for asking.
Otherwise, all I'll
have is my anger.

I am so happy

Pray like Sarah when she held her son Isaac in her arms

My God,
I don't know what to say.
In the midst of my failure,
a gift!
And what a gift it is!

I didn't think it was possible . . .
but then, out of the blue—
happiness!

I think that was you, God.

Forgive me for cheering so loudly.
But I can't be silent
when you've done this for me.

Comfort . . . from God

I rely on God
Pray like Noah after he survived the flood

20

God, you are strong, true, and kind.
I am safe in your hands.
I can live in the shadow of your wings.

Sometimes I am afraid.
Sometimes I see dark clouds,
and lightning tears the sky apart,
and thunder wakes me from my sleep.

But then I think of your words:
As long as the earth remains,
planting and harvesting,
cold and heat, summer and winter,
day and night
will never cease.

And in the sun and clouds
I see the rainbow,
your sign of peace, merciful God,
and your promise.
You want the best for us,
and I can trust you.

I am safe in your hands.
I can live in the shadow of your wings.
Oh strong, true, kind God.

Comfort . . . through baptism

I have a Great Companion
Pray like Samuel, who knew God at a young age

We have a candle, God,
that we sometimes light.
Then we look at photos
of me when I was baptized.

And Mom squeezes my hand.
"Just look at that. You were so young!
You and God have been connected
since then, the small with the big."

I ask her, "So that means nothing bad
can happen to me?"
"It means that whatever happens,"
she says, "you have a Great Companion."

Look at the candle, God!
We are connected!

21

Sorrow . . . after loss

I have doubts
Pray like Job when he tried to understand God

Lord,
when I lose what is dearest to me
and people say:
"It's what God wants,"
I have trouble believing it.

Lord,
when I lose what is dearest to me
and people say:
"It's God testing you,"
I have trouble believing it.

Lord,
when I lose what is dearest to me
and people say:
"Just trust God,"
I don't know
if I can do that.
(Or if I even want to.)

I find comfort

Pray like Job after hearing God's answer

Lord,
when I lose what is dearest to me,
I still feel you close to me.

Lord,
when I lose what is dearest to me,
I still feel you comfort me.

When I lose what is dearest to me,
then I know that you are there, Lord,
and my hope grows
even in the midst of my sorrow.

Compassion ... and helping each other

I am worried

Pray like the disciples when they went out to heal the sick

Dear God, please help!
You give strength to the powerless,
so that they can soar with wings like eagles.
Please come and help!

There's a girl at school
who's too sad and worried
to learn anything.
Or even to smile.

And when she's at home—
well, you know what it's like there.

Jesus, you comfort those who are sad
and make them happy again.
Please come and help!

Holy Spirit, you connect all of us to one another.
Please come and help!

And as for me, I'm going to do what I can.
Please help this girl. And help me too.

I am sad

Pray like Solomon when he was troubled by suffering

Dear God,
what can I do?

What is a small person like me supposed to do
when so many big things go wrong?

I've seen the news on TV.
I've seen the pictures—
pictures I didn't want to see.

And now they're stuck in my head.
And there's nothing I can do.

Please, God,
don't turn away from us!

Comfort all the people who are hurting.
And let peace finally come,
the peace you have promised us.

Envy ... of other people's happiness

I am jealous

Pray like Rachel when she counted Leah's children

When I see them, oh Lord,
when I see how happy they are . . .

Those other kids have so much!
They can do anything they want!
And everything always works out for them.

But me? I just stand on the sidelines.
I can only watch.
Do you know how much that hurts?

Do you hate me?
What makes them better than me?
Why are they more blessed than me?

Why, God?
Do you love them and not me?

I change my mind

Pray like Rachel when she saw Leah's sorrow

What's that I hear, God?
Have you opened my ears?

Those kids I envied—they complain just like me!
They say I have what they want,
and that I can do what they would like to do!
They say that you hate them and love me.

They see things differently than I do.
Have you opened my eyes?

I am amazed and a little comforted.
God, you hear me and see me.
You do love me.

29

Bad mood ... when getting up

I'm feeling grumpy

Pray like Jeremiah when he felt like he was fighting alone

God, I didn't sleep well last night.
And now I don't feel like doing anything.
I don't want to get up at all.
But Mom says I have to.

Everything is going wrong.
Breakfast is cold.
I have a stomachache.
I don't want to wear a sweater. I don't want a scarf.

But then it's too chilly outside. I'm going to catch a cold.
You see, Mom! I told you! It's all your fault!
When I get to the stop, the bus has already left.
Yes, Mom, this is your fault too.

And if it's not your fault, then it's God's!
Hey, God, do you even see all this?
It's not even eight o'clock in the morning,
and the whole day is already ruined.

I'm mad at the whole world today.
I'm not even sorry—
well, I suppose maybe I'm a little sorry . . .
God, you don't have some kind of cure for a
bad mood, do you?

I start to feel better

Pray like Jeremiah when things started to turn around

Well, God, I'm on the bus now.
I'm waiting for your cure.
Someone sits down beside me.
Hey, God, is that because of you?
I close my eyes.
The voice next to me says,
"Don't talk to me.
I had a bad night's sleep."

I don't open my eyes,
but I start grinning.
I reply, "Join the club."

Pain and sickness

I feel pain

Pray like Jesus in the Garden of Gethsemane

Jesus, you experienced
human pain and suffering yourself.

Please listen to me!
Look at me!
I am in pain.

Lord, it hurts so much!
You know how bad it feels.
When will it go away?
When will the pain finally end?

Jesus, who can help me?

I breathe deeply

Pray like the criminal who was crucified with Jesus

Jesus, my brother in pain and suffering,
you look at me from your cross.

It's as if you're saying to me:
You have to get through this.
Breathe deeply. I am here.
I am here, with you,
in the midst of your pain.
And believe me: It will pass.
It will not always be like this.

I can hear you.
I can even feel you here,
a little, maybe.
And in the midst of my pain,
I breathe deeply.

I am sick

Pray like the woman whom Jesus healed

Why is it always me, Jesus?

Just one little breeze, and I get sick.
Just a sneeze from my neighbor, and I catch a bug.
One nasty cold after another.

I am lying in bed.
Not allowed to play outside, not allowed to go to school.
"You need to rest," Mom says.

Do you hear that, God? I'm too sick to do anything!
Jesus, you're the one who needs to do something.
You have the whole world in your hands—including me!
Do you hear me?
Keep me safe in your hands
forever and ever!

I want to be healthy

Pray like the sick man beside the pool of Bethesda

Jesus, my savior,
is it true?

You met people,
people with sickness and pain.
You looked at them and asked:
What do you want me to do for you?

Jesus, didn't you already know?
They wanted to be healthy.
And whole.

I do too, Jesus!
I want to be healthy
and whole.

It's not just a little request.
It's what I really, really want!
Can you do that?
Can you do that for me?

Come on, Jesus,
ask me what I want!
So that I can say to you:
Lord, make me whole!

Jesus, my Savior, save me.

Guilt

I need some help to understand

Pray like Paul when he became a Christian

God, I need your help!
There's something I don't understand.
In Sunday School this morning,
I heard that all people are sinners.
We argue, we fight,
and when I disobey Mom,
or when I lie, even just a little bit . . .
they say that's a sin.

God, can you explain that?
What were you thinking?

You are the one who made us
with minds of our own.
Didn't you think about that?
Do you only want to hear us say
yes and amen?
I can't promise that.

So does that make me *bad*?

God, I need your help!
Please help me be a better person.

I know I won't always be good,
but maybe sometimes I could be a bit calmer,
a bit kinder.

The thing is, God,
I have to keep reminding myself about it.
And then, when you give me a sign
that I messed up,
I have to start all over again.

I am impatient

Pray like Jacob when he wanted his brother's blessing

Dear God in heaven,
I want this so much.

I can't live without it.
I want it so much!

I'll do whatever it takes.
You'll look the other way, won't you?
When I do this one small thing?

You'll understand, won't you?
Because I want this so much.
Even though I know it's not right.

I am freed

Pray like Jacob when God blessed him

God, you are my rock and my hope.
When I admitted my mistake to you
and said I regretted what I did,
you took a sponge
and wiped away the stain of my guilt.

Make amends, you said.
Even if it takes a long time.
I will stay with you and watch you.
I know that you can do it.

39

I'm still running away
from the things I've done.
But I can see hope.
I don't have to be guilty forever.

I thank you, God, and praise you.
Your goodness and mercy
are as vast as heaven.

Self-confidence

I can do this

Pray like David when he protected his sheep

God, come see
what I can do!
I am not as little as people say.

"Do you really want to take on
that much responsibility?"
Mom asked.
"Responsibility for a life,
for a living creature?"

I said yes.
I said yes over and over again.
Until she finally believed me.

And now look: My own pet!
And I'm taking good care of him.
I feed him and give him water.
I make time to play with him.
I never forget about him!

And I gave him a name,
and he knows his name.
I never want to lose him
or let him down.

I can't do this alone

Pray like Saul when he searched for his father's donkeys

Oh God, I don't know what to do!
I'm doing everything I can.
Is that enough?
Is it not enough?
Why not, God, why not?
God, is it my fault
that my pet is lost?
Is it all my fault?
Did I do something wrong?
And how can I make it right, God?

Oh God, please help me find him!
Oh God, what should I do?
Will everything be okay?

I don't have to do this alone

Pray like the father when his prodigal son returned

My pet—he's been found!
I did what I could, and in the end it was enough.

God, do you know what I think?
I didn't do this alone.
I had help with everything I did.

You are the Great Shepherd,
When I was taking care of my pet, you were taking care of me.
And when I slept, you watched him.
You watched over him for me.

Yes, we shared the work.
And yet I believe,
my God, Great Shepherd,
that your care is better than mine.

You watch over both of us—me and my pet.
What can I say, Lord?
I am so grateful.

Amazement ... about creation

I am overwhelmed

Pray like the priests when they recognized God's power as creator

God of heaven and earth,
at night by the campfire,
we see a tent made of stars high above us.
Early in the morning on a mighty mountain,
after struggling our way to the top,
we see the entire world far below us—
fields and meadows, a village, a river . . .

God, I am amazed.
This world is so big and so beautiful!
And it was here long before me!
I didn't create it.
(And neither did Dad or Mom
or any of the great people in this world!)

God of heaven and earth,
when I see a baby—
so tiny, but already a lot like me—
or a puppy,
or a chick in a nest . . .

Oh God, I am amazed.
This world is so big and so beautiful!
And it was here long before me!

Great God of heaven and earth!
You make miracles happen—
and not just big miracles.

You care for
the small and the weak.
You care for
all the plants and animals,
even the nasty ones
that nobody likes.

You care for me.
You have everything in your hands.
You take such great care of us!

Amazement . . . about Jesus

I sit up and listen
Pray like the people who saw the suffering of the beggar Lazarus

Oh, Jesus!
I have heard that the world is a terrible place.
And people say that's just how it is.
There's nothing to be done about it.

Oh, Jesus! I look around,
and it seems like they are right.
I see the homeless man in his dirty clothes
outside the rich people's window.
I can't help him.
That's what I tell myself.

Oh, Jesus! I hear that you
treat the world with love.
Does that actually change anything?
They say you reach out your hand to those in need,
and the rich seem poor beside you.

Oh, Jesus! Does that really help?
Those stories about you—
they're like a light
in the middle of the dark night.

I see light

Pray like the people who saw Jesus's miracles

Wow, Jesus!
It's so amazing what you dare to do!
You seek out those in need.
You hold out your hand to the people who are sick.
Everyone avoids these people,
but not you!

Jesus, how are you able to care for those in need?
It's not something I could do too, is it?

Arguing

I am right

Pray like Elijah when he fled to Mound Horeb

I got in an argument, God.
I was really upset.
I knew that I was right.

I knew you were on my side.
I was sure of it.

But my friends got mad,
and now half the class is against me.
Go on, tell them that I'm right!

You're not saying anything.
You're not stepping in to help.
Don't leave me standing here all alone.

I want to be friends again

Pray like Elijah when he heard God in a gentle whisper

I won the argument, God.
No one could disagree with me.
Everyone fell silent.

I yelled until I was exhausted.
Come on, God, say that I was right!

I won the argument, God.
But I still didn't convince anyone.
Now I'm all alone.

I yelled until I was exhausted, God.
Come on, say that I was right!

I won the argument, God.
But now I'm having doubts. Was I right?

I yelled until I was exhausted, God.
From now on, please give me peace.

Mourning . . . for a grandparent

I don't want this to happen
Pray like Joseph when Jacob was sick and dying

God, you can do anything!
Please make Grandpa well again!
He's been in bed for days,
and Mom says he doesn't want to keep on going.

But God, how can that be?
How can he not want to keep going?

I need him!
He reads me bedtime stories.
And he can do math
much better than I can . . .

I am furious

Pray like Naomi when she lost everything

God, why didn't you help?
You were supposed
to make Grandpa better!

But you didn't do anything.
And so things got worse,
and now Grandpa is gone!

God, I'm really angry at you!
Why did you let him die?
After I had asked and prayed . . .

I don't really know . . .

Pray like Abraham when Sarah died

Hey God, wherever you're hiding . . .
Mom says Grandpa was tired.
Mom says Grandpa didn't want to tell any more stories.
He'd even stopped enjoying math.

Mom says Grandpa really loved me,
but still he couldn't stay.

53

Mom says you did the right thing,
that you took him into your arms.
And she says that's where he is now.
In your arms.

I don't know, God, if I believe that,
or if I think that was really the right thing.
Or if I understand at all.
Mom says it's going to be okay.
But she has tears in her eyes when she says it.

I am sad

Pray like Martha and Mary when their brother Lazarus died

God, with your open arms,
can you give Grandpa a hug from me?
Please tell him that I miss him!

Tell him I have his old book of stories.
And his gardening gloves too.
Mom wanted to throw them out!
But I saved them.

Grandpa, I miss you!
I can still see you,
sometimes, when I close my eyes.
I can still smell you—
tobacco, coffee, and medicine.
Your voice, though, I can't hear that anymore . . .

God, with your open arms,
give Grandpa a hug from me. And maybe . . .
could you spare a hug for me too?

Overwhelmed . . . by a task

It's too much for me

Pray like Jonah when he ran away from God's command

Oh God, I don't feel brave enough to do this!

They gave me this task.
They trust me to do it.
But what about how I feel?
They didn't ask me.

If I take on this task,
I might fail!
I might look stupid!

Oh God, why me?
I'd rather pass it on to someone else.

To someone who has
more courage and strength than I do.

I'm stuck

Pray like Jonah inside the whale

Oh God, it feels like
I keep running into a brick wall.
This task that I didn't want,
I can't get rid of it!

No one else wants it,
and no one else wants to help me!

God, please help me!
Take this burden from me.
I don't want it, I never wanted it!

What did you say?
Okay, maybe at first I wanted to try.

Maybe at first I thought I could do it,
but I didn't really think it through!

What did you say?
Yes, I know. You won't abandon me.
You are by my side.
You will give me all the strength I need.

Okay, then, God—you and me!
We can do this together!

57

Impatience . . . for the kingdom of heaven

I am restless

Pray like the disciples when they were waiting for the kingdom to come

Jesus, your words make me happy—
your words about the kingdom of heaven,
about life as it should be,
about God's faithful presence!

Your words make me glad.
They make me think.
I like to hear them.

But I would also like to see
your words come true.

Your kingdom come, we pray,
as you said we should.
Yes, I want your kingdom to come.

Jesus, you made the blind see
and the lame walk,
and you gave relief to those
who were discouraged!

They make me restless, those deeds.
They feel like a challenge to me.

I would like to be able
to do those things too.
Maybe one day? Maybe even today?

Your will be done, we pray,
as you said we should.

Yes, your will be done.

Taking responsibility ... for others and for the world

I ask about right and wrong
Pray like the Israelites when they heard God's command

Dear God,
there's a new kid
at school.
She's a bit different than us.
Not exactly cool,
if you know what I mean . . .

Dear God,
I want to ask you something.
Is it fair
that none of us
talk to her?

Is it fair
that no one wants to sit by her,
and no one wants to help?

Does that sound right to you?
I mean, I don't really think I need
to reach out to her.
I already have good friends.
And yet . . .

Dear God, I see
how sad she is.
That surely can't be right.

I ask about good and evil
Pray like Habakkuk when he called out to God

God, up there on your cloud,
That's how I painted you in my picture,
up on a cloud.

I don't want you to get
the wrong idea, though.
I didn't paint you,
not you, not quite.
I just painted how I want you to be.

I want you to see what's happening,
and hear our prayers.
I want you to act, to help, to save.
And give bad people what they deserve.
Be King, and be Judge!

I have seen things on TV—
the things that bad people do.
I've seen how they build weapons.
I've seen how they fight wars.

I've seen how they abuse animals,
keeping them in small cages
without any light.

I hear about how they spoil everything—
the air and the water, the mountains and
the valleys.

Every moment, a child dies.
Every moment, a plant, an animal
leaves the earth forever.

But it's your earth, God!
You're the one who made it!
Please come down from your cloud
and judge them!
Stop their wickedness!

I am so sad, God,
I lie awake and wonder:
What's going to happen, God?

How long are you going to just watch?

I receive an answer

Pray like Gideon when he heard God's voice

That God on the cloud,
the one I painted recently . . .
He has two arms and two hands.

And those hands, God,
those hands are open.

I dreamed, God,
that you spoke to me.

And your hands, God,
your hands were open.

You said that it's not enough
just to see wickedness.
You said that it's not enough
just to recognize injustice.

But God, I'm just a kid!
What am I supposed to do?

Am I supposed to save the earth,
to end wars, to feed the hungry?
To open up the cages and free the animals?
To make the air and water
clean again?

I dreamed, God,
that you spoke to me.

And your hands, God,
your hands took mine.

63

You are not alone, you said.
Believe me, my child.
Questions and prayers can help a lot.

Then, dear Lord, I woke up.
And I wonder: What now?

I take action

Pray like the Good Samaritan Jesus spoke about

God, you are down here among your people!
I've painted a new picture of you now!
You are like fire in our hearts,
like wind in our hair—
a wind that blows like a gentle nudge.

I felt that nudge
when I got to school this morning
and saw the new girl.

She was standing there all alone.
And my friends were sitting
on the other side of the playground.

"Hey! Over here!" they shouted to me.
And that was when I felt the nudge.
I went over to the new girl instead
and said hello.

The new girl is a little different, God.
But you know,
when we're laughing and having fun,
the new girl is just like me—
just another kid.

Taking responsibility . . . for our own actions

I'm not sure

Pray like Moses when he went to Pharaoh (and things got worse)

Listen, God.
Something happened.
And now I don't know
if I did the right thing.

I saw it happen.
There was a bully.
And a victim.
There's no doubt about that.

I saw the whole thing.
And then . . . I snitched.

That's what they call it.
But that's not how I meant it.
I thought, *I have to speak up.*

That was the right thing to do, wasn't it?
You said that it was.
And so did all your prophets.

But I'm worried
it didn't make anything better.
Maybe it even made things worse.

Listen, God.
Is it possible to do a good thing
that turns out badly?
And what then?
Is everything all my fault?

I calm down
Pray like the people whom Jesus reassured

Ah, Jesus!
The boy I tried to help
smiled at me today.
And later he even laughed.
Will everything be okay after all?

Ah, Jesus!
Was it you?
Did you help everything work out?
Or was it just a question of time?
Maybe both.
Maybe it was the two of us
together?

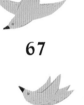

Ah, Jesus!
I want to be more patient.
You say: *Don't worry so much.*
You are not alone.

Yes, Jesus,
I think that helps.

Trust . . . in the creator

I know that I was made by God

Pray like Adam and Eve when they experienced the miracle of life

God, you are a great artist!
How did you make this happen?

My baby cousin there in the crib . . .
how did she come into the world?

They tell me that my aunt
gave birth to her.
They tell me that she's a mix of
both my aunt and uncle.
They say that it's completely ordinary.

But I'm not sure about that, God.
It isn't ordinary.
They have tears in their eyes.
They're amazed—just like I am.

God, you are a great artist!
How did you make this happen?

I look at my reflection in the mirror.
How did I become who I am?

They tell me that Mom
gave birth to me.
They tell me that I'm a mix of
both Mom and Dad.
Of course I know that.

And yet—that's not everything.
I know you were involved.

I know that your hand shaped me.
I know that you breathed life into me.

You made me—a miracle!
And you entrusted me to my parents.

I feel small (and big)

Pray like Peter when he recognized his own weaknesses

God, you are a great artist.
Sometimes I can hardly believe it—
that you created me!
That you really want me!

You know that I am not always good.
I get mad a lot,
and then I scream and shout.
(And afterwards I can't even
remember why.)
I can be unfair,
and sometimes I'm really selfish.

One time, God, I opened
the doors of the Advent calendar,
all of them at once.
That's how impatient I am.

Oh, if you only knew!
But then I think: *Of course you know!*
You're the one who made me!

What were you thinking
when you made me?
Can you really put up with me?
I thank you from the bottom of my heart.

A thought just came to me.
I think it came from you.
You made me who I am,
and you help me to become better.

Anger . . . about unfairness

I am angry
Pray like Martha when Mary didn't want to help her

She's so mean, God!
My little sister!

She takes my things.
She doesn't tell me, and she doesn't ask.
Sometimes she even breaks them.
Or doesn't give them back at all!

She's always up to something.
And Mom doesn't even notice!
Mom thinks she's an angel!

But you know everything.
You know the truth.
Be the Judge.
Whose side are you on?

I am jealous

Pray like Joseph's brothers when Joseph got special treatment

72

God, oh God!
It's him again, my big brother!

He gets away with everything!
He always goes too far,
and no one stops him!
He's so cool and so big,
and he gets whatever he wants.

But not me!
I only hear:
"Go to sleep."
"Do your homework."
"Be quiet!"

I can't take it anymore.
And do you know what the worst thing is?

He teases me on purpose,
about the very thing that
bothers me so much—
that he's allowed to do everything,
and I'm not allowed to do anything at all!

I have time to think

Pray like Joseph's brothers when they made up with Joseph

Oh God, why are you silent?
It's really quite easy:
Stand by me, God,
I am your child!

Oh God, you are silent,
and I have time to think.
Sometimes, some days—
my siblings are really nice.

Then I love them.
And they love me too.

Oh, God!
They're your children too,
just like I am.

73

Doubts . . . about God's justice

I don't understand
Pray like the disciples when they thought they would drown

God, you are mysterious.
And I don't understand!

Why do people have to die?
It's so random.
One person is struck by lightning,
and another is not.
One dies in an accident,
and another survives.

God, you are hidden.
And I don't understand!

Why do some people suffer
and others don't?
One person becomes sick,
and another gets better.
One is born weak,
and another is happy and strong.

God, it doesn't seem fair.
But then I ask myself:
What would be fair?

I think I know . . .

Pray like Solomon when he saw the evil in the world

God, you have the world in your hands.
That's what they say.

I've thought about this for a long time.
I've thought about
what we suffer in life:
Death. We know that one day we will all die.
Pain. Injuries happen, and they hurt.
Injustice. Not everyone is happy.
Guilt. We all do things we shouldn't do.
War. People kill others, instead of getting along.

God, you have the world in your hands.
Surely you could make it better.
I've thought about it,
and I ask you from the bottom of my heart:

Lord, please just stop the suffering!

I know my path

Pray like Paul when he wrote about faith and living on earth

God, you can be so difficult, so hidden.
I have struggled with you.
I have accused you
of not doing enough.
Of not hearing when I call you.
Of not stepping in when there's trouble.

God, you are so mysterious, so wise.
I had a dream where I was in heaven.
And everything was perfect.

But in my dream, before long,
I started to hate heaven.
It seemed . . . boring.

Did you make me this way, God?
So restless and impatient?

Did you make us this way,
so hungry to take in all of life?
Happiness and sorrow,
joy and suffering?

Wise King, Bright Light,
I ask for forgiveness.

Earth should be earth.
And heaven can come later.
And yet its light leads us on.
With your help,
I will trust you and do what I can now.

References

79

80